some kind of miracle

miracle

LAURA EIGENMANN

some kind of miracle

LAURA EIGENMANN

**Bibliographic information by the German National Library
(DNB):** The German National Library lists this publication in the
National Bibliography; detailed bibliographic data is available
on the Internet at dnb.dnb.de.

Cover Design by: Núria Solsona

Illustrations by: Sophie Graff

Text Design by: Laura Eigenmann

Print and Publication by: BoD – Books on Demand,
Norderstedt

ISBN: 978 3 75261 256 1

to the dreamer in you
in me
in all of us

Content

If you want me to
I will be the one
That is always good
And you'll love me too
But you'll never know
What I feel inside
That I'm really bad
Little trouble girl

Little Trouble Girl by Sonic Youth, 1995

INTRODUCTION

Words are my salvation

I was four years old when I was first able to put my life's most essential cornerstones down in writing: Mama, Papa, Laura. Written in capital letters and with an inverted R, they laid the ground for a magnitude of stories that would accompany my loneliest childhood days and follow me into late adolescence. I had always been an unusual girl. When the young and naive affection I offered the world was ridiculed and rejected time and time again, I turned pain into beauty by transforming it into rhymes. Realizing that the world didn't hold a place for the colorfulness that was my soul, I used my imagination to invent a self that could – and would – be accepted.

Convinced that everything – *anything* – must and will come to an end and that people will always leave, I became voraciously hungry for experiences. I aimed to continually get to the bottom of what connected us as humans and in such kept drowning myself in everyone seemingly offering me a place to rest my head. Eventually, I gave my heart to someone who could not only truly understand the dustiest corners of my mixed-up soul but ultimately also stripped me of everything she could find there. I didn't know it back then, but her leaving left me bereft of my writing. Lost for words, I had lost myself.

The years that followed were marked by self-medicated numbness and a quest for vengeance so ferocious it would not only destroy the sensitive girl inside of me but everyone else that dared to come too close to her. On the outside, I grew up to be an independent so-called successful woman, but deep down my brokenness prevented me from the very connection I had once so desperately searched for.

They say it takes getting everything you ever wanted and then losing it to know what true freedom is. To me, that meant meeting the person that would untangle the madness that haunted me and then watching my darkness slowly but ever so surely break him. His love for me was like Icarus' devotion to the sun – pure, painful and ultimately fatal. Its honesty cracked my heart open, shining a light into the ugliest rooms within myself and brutally forcing me to take responsibility for what I had buried there. Sadly, it took me too long to understand that this, too, had been a gift.

At last, the downfall turned out to be my redemption. Re-membering the girl I used to be had set me free. Not long after, my heart was captivated by a love so solid and nurturing, it could convince me that sometimes, people *do* stay. He offered me something no one ever had before: hope. By his side, I was able to soften up my defenses and at the same time reconnect to the untamed wildness that accounts for the very essence of my being. Feeling safely grounded by his presence, I ventured out into the unknown. Once I rediscovered myself, words came back to me.

And, oh boy – did they come back to me!

For the first time in what seemed like forever, I allowed myself to be seen by others – if only a chosen few – vulnerably and openly. Whenever we granted each other access to uncharted terrain, we got the chance to recognize ourselves through the eyes of another, deconstructing our reality and reconstructing it accordingly. I learned that it is never too late to be the person you want to be. That – even if loneliness is indeed the human condition – people who can *truly* grasp your complexity exist; you just need to look a little bit further than what meets the eye. I saw how desire can be born out of the very rawness we so desperately try to conceal. And I discovered my heart rejoicing at the profound connection it can form to another human being. I let constructive pain be my teacher so that I could admit to my limitations, and – ultimately – allow myself to fall in love.

Today I know writing holds the key to my salvation.

As long as I write, I live.

What you hold in your hands is a journey to finding my own voice, guided and inspired by the words of other artistic souls that have come before me. It is dedicated to them, to you and to the us we have created. May we encounter a love in one another that finds a way to the places within us that we want to keep hidden, the places where we fear we're not good enough, and prove us wrong. Maybe that's when we will finally realize that we all are some kind of miracle.

the prologue

---

to the ones breaking

Part I

hardship had become my teacher
the year when resilience had merged with my limits
and heaviness had shown me how to rise again

when I could handle it least, I wondered:
oh simplicity, where had she gone?
could I rely on complexity to take her seat?
take over guidance and make me complete?

I learned to cultivate loneliness
let it tunnel into me and allow my soul room to grow
I learned never to hope to outgrow it
never ask anyone to lift me up when I'm low
I learned nobody can fill that space
and that that space over our lives
can remind us to forget the pain

I now know the lessons will come back tomorrow
if they are not learned today

now I'll choose empathy over disconnection
courage over what's known and certain
I'll toast to freedom over perfection
doing the work over complaints about the burden

they say nothing I've learned can prepare me
for everything else that needs learning

so,
tell me
when are you going to let me in?
when are we there?
when can we begin?

the first truth is easy
  the lover wants what he can't have
  it's by definition impossible for him
  to have what he wants
  if – as soon as it is had – it is no longer wanting

the second truth is known
  to love is to battle
  when two look at each other and see
  the world changes
  to love is to bet
  a bet placed on freedom
  not my own
  but the freedom of the other

the third truth is simple
  gone for now feels a lot like gone for good

the spoken truths crack the concrete
in our throats and release what isn't ours to keep
we water beliefs that can only breathe life right back into us

so,
tell me
who do you want to be?
who do you want to trust?
and do you think it could be me?

and if it's true
that nothing I've learned can prepare me
and all will always be returning
unprotect me and have me start burning
have impatience consume me while yearning
for everything more I could see
it could be a reflection of me
in you, in me, in you …
or all just a deja vu?

let me untangle the madness that haunts you
let me break you, so you can be open
open you, so you can expand
expand you, so you can create space
to invite more love in

let's fall apart, so our pieces can come together
and be rearranged again
let's believe in the wild possibility of our own impact
and knowing
                    you are enough

let this be more than just waiting
more than a *save me* to strangers

I'm coming back to that memory
to the meaning of a moment shared
I weigh it and that's when I realize
authenticity was key

so here is the deepest secret nobody knows

my head was feeling scared
but my heart was feeling *free*

Part II

so much deafening silence stretching above me
around me and inside of me
your presence is still lingering
it's filling me up with words demanding rupture
has the silence itself brought about this rapture?
I let myself be captured
and immersed in it
     drowned
there's never enough to be found, to be unbound

I'm not driven by instinct but drawn in by significance
persuaded by meaning, escaping indifference
I guess it's never too late to go beyond your own surface
shattering beliefs, finding your purpose

the deeper I get, the rawer I feel
     it's getting real
          bursting another wall
               I can see that there's more
        and it's calling me back to before

I'm obsessive and reckless and I like it this way
did we only come out to play?
is this the real life or is it just fantasy?
I asked you to join me; alone, I can't cope

    I built a window into daring and ultimately *hope*

now I dare you to move
to let your world be transformed
don't say you weren't warned

it is always a choice
between the red and the blue
the old and the new

how desperate are you for freedom?
is the truth always brutal?
do you prefer blissful oblivion?

what are we here for if not for this?
you know, there's no inherent meaning
only the meaning we give

and I give it all when I'm giving
won't give up on risking and living
      and feeling
           and relying on somebody else
              so to feel in control
      while losing myself

you can take what you get
I can live with regret

    as long as we let ourselves *interact* and *connect*

there once was a time when the one I betrayed most
    was *myself*

because I had lost touch
the pain had just been too much
I couldn't handle the beast
and how she had fooled me
she had told me she loved me
when really she had ruled me

see,
the experience numbed me and it blinded my view
and it made me do things I never meant to do
the day innocence was lost and all things changed
I turned to damaging decisions
that lead to lies and mistakes

so now, I'm so hungry, almost insatiable
for something with truth
something unchangeable
now I'm laid bare like an open-ended nerve
now I know we accept the love we think we deserve

if one thing I can promise
it's that you're not on a pedestal
and I will anyhow show you
that you're fucking incredible

so with this one I toast to the *hopeless romantics*
to the lonely, the broken, the fearless, the frantic
to the *yous* whose secrets I will treasure and keep
to the songs that we play and that put us to sleep

they say there's a space between   trigger
        and
                    reaction
and in this space lies our power to choose
it's our reaction that determines our growth
and our freedom
and sometimes it all depends
on how much we have to lose

so I thought about us
and the nature of companionship
and how beginnings hold the promise of a story untold
and I wondered if sometimes
hitting a plateau
is really just another word
for putting on a show

and even though we know
that change is inevitable
it takes time to adjust
and so I take a leap of faith
into honesty and trust

and when I reach over and take your hand
the silence in my head turns into sound
and where once I was lost
I can now feel the ground
and where once I was scared
I open my heart

     and what once felt like the *ending*
      suddenly feels like the *start*

Part III

hoping to meet my kind
in a world that deems the
unsophisticated empty rooms
they call souls
    normality
a world that calls numbness
    sanity
creating safe spaces
for their
    victim mentality

it all seems to be a mission
with a clearly hopeless outcome
but paradise might be found
just behind the highest mountain
and
              if it were *easy*
            it would be *worthless*

so,
maybe I have to fight for it
before I can finally let myself

dissolve
        into
                the
                        infinite

what do you consider the chances
to filter out
one piece of truth
from all their small talk?
all those artless words
they use to dodge my onslaught
they're chilling me to the bone
between that and solitude
I'll always choose being alone

even though
when distraction lost effect
it paved the way for agony to come back

so,
what if I don't miss *you*
but how you made me *feel*?
or I just loved to be challenged
to be honest
to be real
and
they are all blinded
they all can't see through
the smoke's too thick
I'm just *too wicked*

and that leads me back to you

your presence warms my heart
no matter how far away you are
it's just comforting to know
in the nuances we're similar
my kind exists
and thinks of me
even if only from time to time
I can't forget just how sublime
we were when you were mine

no wonder they can't touch me
as long as I am in control
control makes you indifferent
and then it eats you whole
playfulness is only deep
when it's understood
then it distinctively teaches you
the difference between
        I *could*
and   I *would*

my intellectual conviction
is basically worth nothing
I can't comprehend
what doesn't reflect
it doesn't matter how much they are loving
me

so,
how long do you think I can sit
with the pain of the mundane?
impressing yet another simpleton
while I'm sipping on champagne

that sounds like fun, right?
enjoy it while you can!
meanwhile their souls will still be vacant
but looking pretty on instagram

I'm sure you know that feeling
when someone looks beyond the bullshit
    right
        into
           you
and you almost have a heart attack

it makes me think about the plastic bag
and how you just might be the end of me

I guess at least it gave me poetry
and an ambition to create
and so I creatively build my castle
while I dare you to

      just wait

we keep this friendship alive
and thrive on each other's love
we laugh laugh laugh at all plot twists
written by this guy above
about a world
that calls numbness
sanity
a world that deems
emptiness
normality

so probably I should be grateful
for the few humans I've got
stay humble
generous
and open
and reserve you a little spot

a cozy one
right by my side
lean into it

and
      enjoy
            the
                  ride

the lessons

to the ones becoming

to keep balance, you must keep moving

back to
  when I told myself
  everything good takes time
  and I wasn't even sure
  how much I believed it
  how much I believed myself
  how much I believed
  that I could walk a path unwalked
  unbreak a core so broken
  that it would take a life
  to restore the billion pieces
  to rebuild the very essence
  of my fractured self

back to
  when I tried to step forward
  into the light
  and to forget
  the shadows of the reminiscence
  that was my past
  the blackness that was my outlook
  the phantoms that were haunting
  my every motion
  a bulk of darkness
  walking with me
  at all times

back to
    the initial days of grief
    when I knew
    I needed to move on
    but I was unable to move
    for even breathing exhausted me
    my lungs collapsing
    at the very thought of having to take another one
    another breath
    another confirmation
    that
     life
          goes
              on
    that I still live
    that I still *feel*
    no matter my trials to numb
    whatever parts of me
    that craved apathy
    so tirelessly

back to
> the moment of realization
> that life waits for nobody
> that old lovers
> will fold into new relationships
> and start different journeys without you
> that *hello*s will turn into
> *I haven't seen you for a while*
> that friendships turn into love
> and love into something more
> or
> nothing at all
> that the hurt
> that filled my heart
> has to eventually spill over
> to make room
> for more love to come in

and when I kept walking
I finally understood
that those who broke me
will in the end return to the place
where they had left me

only to find that I am no longer standing there
waiting for them

whatever is difficult is good

exhausting my tenderness
embodying her rejection
hoping she'd be coming
waiting for her to be texting
and all because she said she would
  whatever is difficult is good

cutting memories into skin
for lack of an escape
the hurt allows the anger in
when she arrives, it'll be too late
cause she don't treat me like she should
  whatever is difficult, is good

rising up from heaviness
being my own best friend
I finally won the battle
that brought the war to an end
and I hadn't thought I could
  whatever is difficult is good

praising independence
painting the town red
you think she got the best of me
but that's not what I said
why am I so misunderstood?
  whatever is difficult is good

living on the brink of life
mastering the fire
went walking on a tightrope
now go on, call me a liar
I embraced temptation and I withstood
whatever is difficult is good

carrying the consequences
consistent with my views
telling her how I really felt
got nothing else to lose
now I watch her stand right where I stood
whatever is difficult is good

beauty can be born out of pain

I want to tell you about how the worst parts of me
are also the birthplace of the best parts

how if you dig deep enough and look beyond what you see
you'll eventually discover my graveyards

where everyone's buried, I have ever broken
in ways much worse than you'd guess

while I was battling the fields of a war unspoken
trying to love myself regardless

the echo of their words resounds within the void
of the place where my heart used to be

and it's actually there, among those ruins destroyed
that there's space enough for my truth to roam free

so I let thunderstorms fill me inexorably
because you know I'm not scared of their fire

as the hollows they cause are the depths within me
where you'll find meaning, my guts, my desire

it's that room that every once in a while
I let you sneak into just for a peek

and the rawness you taste there brings out that smile
because you love to play hide and seek

isn't it therefore true after all
that beauty can be born out of pain

and that what made me crazy, stumble and fall
is at the same time what kept me sane

I write

I write
because I have to create a world
in which I can live
as I can not live in any of the worlds offered to me
I can not breathe
reign
and recreate myself in any of those worlds

I write
to lure and enchant you
you and others
to serenade the lovers
to taste life twice
in the moment
and in retrospect
to render all of it eternal
despite the disconnect

I write
to expand myself when I feel lonely
as by writing to you
you are always here with me
an incarnation of my inner universe
messages between the lines
that I can't express with words

I write
for too many centuries
women have been busy being muses to the artists
but now we claim the artistic work for ourselves
turning others into our muses
so I write to heal our bruises
be self-soothing
to the degree that comes naturally to you

I write
to claim your attention
to tunnel a way into you
a you that is yet undefined
and affected by the meaning
of what this writing has to offer

I write
to feel like I am good enough
to fall in love
and find that place we have been dreaming of

an ode to atticus

my mind is a wasteland
I saw the storm in your eyes
I'm just a girl
maddened by her delirious wish
to be satisfied

I tell myself
there are places in the world
that aren't made out of stone
there are answers to be found there
to questions still unknown
there's something inside all of us
that they can't get to
they can't reach

there might be a way to *redemption*
through the *lessons* we teach

follow the yellow bricks
and you might just find peace
childishly believe
that even if people leave
they might eventually reappear
and be honest and sincere

my mind's dancing alive
to the symphonies of the dark
mad to live
mad to burn
like the ardor in my heart

love could be labeled poison
I'd drink it anyway
without a doubt
standing on the buffet of life
I'm always scared of missing out

in the center of this hurricane
you'll find serenity and calm
you can rest your head beside me
I'll protect you and keep you warm

when everything comes crashing down
my words will give me wings
they say

poets are *fools*
until they are *kings*

love her but leave her wild

intelligence and wit
had drawn me in defenselessly
         trapped me
    entangled me
in the purity
of his company

so innocent and yet
defiant maybe
to what I had held true
while I mastered the game
he defined the rules anew

a love so impossible
suicidal from the start
and while we both burned out
we stayed connected heart to heart

deep down I was always sure
that I could never live up
to all the promises I had made
to all the dreams that we had touched

the *golden cage* became too small
for such a wild and untamed soul
I would always try to escape
until he finally let me go

it takes a life to become young

you say it's going to take you a while
and a little while longer
to really embrace feeling like 18
to lose your *escapism*
and resolve your most-hard wired scheme
of being drawn back to complacence
drowning in your own *tragedy*

every time I look at you these days
I see you change into someone new
and I realized
that it is quite a mesmerizing sight
to stare into the chocolate-brown sea of your eyes
and get lost there

I'm always hoping to capture something real
figuring out your focal point
that remains unchanged
independently from what you might feel

so I try to come up with ways
to explain the
        space
                between us
and deal with the changes of light
our relationship in constant shift
smooth on some days and on others a fight

and I'm pulling
        alluring
           seducing you
a you complete
yet undefined
seeking ways to solve the puzzle inside
of your heart
your body and mind

and every time I think I might be there
you change the rules and move on
like a constant game of truth or dare
which I see has only just begun

so whenever I get down to challenging you
how brave do you think you can be?
there's this
      moment of silence
           between us
and then you turn the narrative around on me

instead of asking then
I will solemnly promise
that what you'll find in me
you can keep
and when you finally let yourself hold me
you will be held

and when you fall into deep
you will feel what I've felt
and see through my eyes
a world waiting to be *intensified*

you say it's going to take you a while
and a little while longer
and that at the same time we'll have to be quick
but see, there's a catch-22
between honesty and playing a trick
on you

for I can play this game
but what for?
I'd much rather go and explore
the depth within you
and lose sight of the shore

so,
I won't stop until we're done
and they say *it takes time to get young*

the promise

having you stand
on a rock so inherently
part of nature
so natural
so *genuine*
that the very genuineness
of that moment
was reflected
in that promise
so unplanned for
like a life
bound by the promise
of that very moment
and yet
                              disconnected
by just the same life
and its pain

how dancing
could feel so free
and yet we got each other
in all these chains
we never anticipated
that it could be us
that it won't be us
that we couldn't trust
that promise

of a life yet to be told
a treasure to hold
a risk to be taken
so bold
that we would laugh
at all odds
laugh at all gods
that would question
our love

how can it be
that a belief
so naive
can ring so true
to me
to you
to the us we've created
and built together
into a family
so fundamental
to that promise
that only
another family built
could destroy it

I'm telling them a tale of us
and I haven't quite decided yet
how it will end
for the end might be
a beginning anew
a rekindling of sparks
and yet I doubt
I always do

but doubters are just *dreamers*
with broken hearts

part I

part II

to keep balance,
you must keep
moving

whatever is difficult is good

beauty can be born out of pain

an ode to atticus

the promise

the moments

her

jealousy

the lover

to the ones dreaming

a good muse

a good muse
offers you
storms at night
to make you want to kiss
the shore
and ache for more
than just words
to unravel
the dustiest corners
of your mixed-up soul
and give up control
to lean in
letting yourself be
consumed
by her tenderness
embracing
the opportunity
to be adventurous
trusting that...

...in the morning
she will give you
calm seas
a chance to breathe
and consolidate
all ambiguity
of the night before
not asking more
of you but faith
in her
and her power to save
whatever parts of you
that need salvation
a different outlook
or resolved temptation
she gives you serenity
and a place to rest
your head
your beating heart
on her chest

the morning

it's both
a blessing and a curse
to feel everything
so very deeply
and with some tiredness
and strained bones
I immerse myself
completely
into the *wild unknown*
the dreaminess
of a lazy sunday morning
it's early winter
but it rather feels
like summer's gentle warming
her light shines through
the cracks of my
imbalanced precondition
and movements
search for company
almost like on a mission
a journey to forgiveness
love
audacity
and hope
a dream of places far away
outlandish
and remote

I freeze the moment
so it exists
as long as I don't overflow
enters my mind
reaches my heart
and paints me in *indigo*
there's no tomorrow
only gravity
chaining me to now
we won't regress
we'll only long for
anything that we allow
you wish for *secrets*
some you want shared
and saying no
has never been so sweet
yes you can trust me
and I can trust that you'll
play
       pause
            and repeat
no echo of
decisions taken
for whatever they may be
I guess it's true
that I found *you*
when I went looking out for *me*

what if

what if
> we come full circle
> when *ambivalence*
> is *overcome*
> once we engage
> the uncertain
> and there's no place
> else to run
> to
> no place else
> you can hide
> will you then
> turn the tide
> and confide
> in me

what if
> I can't deny that
> *violating prohibitions*
> is my own personal
> favorite poison
> even in times
> of great ambition
> of great responsibility
> to hell with what society
> expects of us
> or thinks of me

what if
    the search for power
    is an endlessly
    charming game
    we said we stopped
    but we still encounter
    the same old pattern
    just with a new name
    maybe
    within a new frame
    and if you look closely
    you'll see that
    it's almost
    one and the same

what if
    we'll invest some energy
    into some distance
    into the wait
    I guess we'll only end up *longing*
    for everything we can *anticipate*
    and meanwhile
    we'd be throwing all our secrets
    into the sky like dreams
    because you know for lovers
    time is measured in the in-betweens

the moments

close your eyes
let the silence linger between us
for a moment longer than usual
let it guide you back to a reminiscence
a recollection of intensity

one is a safeguarded memory
of a moment so honest and pure
of being pulled tight and held close
feeling protected and secure

it was the first time that
you weren't the one to let go
and for a while there you became *softer*
than the man I used to know

this fuzzy feeling around your heart
hold onto it
it is your own
and holds the power to transform you
keeping you safe and warm

in the aftermath I sat there
alone and silent with eyes closed
let electricity run through my veins
enjoyed what we call *firesmoke*

in another one of these fragments
there's your voice
on the other side of somewhere
the tone filled with genuine *honesty*
different from the one known to me

no sense of the glass walls shielding you
and maybe even a trace of the boy
running the streets of an *endless city*
his heart filled with excitement and joy

we shared an understanding of the meaning
of an impossible love and its pain
how even if we give it our all
our struggle can still be in vain

my fingers wandered slowly
over the soft texture of your skin
up   and up again
          and down
until the end where we begin

that night you took my hand
and led me to the edge
let electricity run through our veins
and left me *the sea as a pledge*

and when you now open your eyes
you'll realize to no surprise
what makes us fall
the one underlying reason for it all

bloody *authenticity*
every time she holds the key
the key that sets us free
and had us see
the core of what makes you you
and what makes me me

about freedom

city of high lights
the sound of the sea

        crispy fall mornings
        cold air on reddened cheeks

freedom so inconsistent
with boundaries chosen

        an honest resurrection
        and a moment frozen in time

wind in my hair
sun rising over skies

        a new hello
        and endless goodbyes

a story of love
the ending unknown

        walking these streets
        that smell just like home

on top of a hill
the meaning of time

        hands held after midnight
        my heart drenched in wine

and at the end
when I finally fall

        a silent confirmation
        that *Bob Dylan knew it all*

the desire

to the ones burning

say

say you know
to discern right from wrong
being weak
from being strong
having a place to live
from knowing you belong

say you are aware
of the value of time
of a rhyme so sublime
as the price of a kiss
conveying the real meaning of
I miss you

say you believe
that what inspires
rewires
that what burns like fire
can hold magic
and even birth desire

say you want
to unbalance your life
to fight for what's right
to call me friend
but keep me closer
all through the night

hold me, thrill me, kiss me, kill me

hold me
      like I am the last straw anchoring you
      to any worldly sensation proving you exist
      and I promise you'll find within that embrace
      all the things you think you miss

thrill me
      like there's no amount of risk and daring
      that shall ever be deemed too much
      and I promise to ensure electricity
      every single time we touch

kiss me
      like the physicality of my lips
      is the only evidence you have
      that this moment is real
      and I promise to guide you to my secret place
      where all your hurt can heal

kill me
      like a man that can't bear the thought
      of any other man
      ever touching my skin
      and I promise to teach you the value of loss
      before I finally let you in

her

the way she moves, eyes closed, in the zone
is the movement of someone owning their own
playing alone to a person unknown to me
hidden from the frame that I see

and I like to imagine she knows I am here
she's sensing my presence
feeling me near
and everything is allowed
just for tonight
as we turn down the light
and lose sight of what's right
or wrong or uncalled for
or what could destroy
the fragile balance of this life with a boy
that is giving me
everything   *anything*
but not this
the taste of her kiss
the guilty pleasure of a body that's not his

the meaning of a closeness only we understand
and while I'm looking for *otherness*
in the palm of her hand
I rediscover myself
lost in her gaze
lustfulness coming   *and going*   in waves

her body is home
to a temple I kneel at
to a world that I know
a world that was mine just a moment ago
so I gladly sacrifice all I have to give

        cause there's something in her *tenderness*
            that makes me want to *live*

and with every move, I beg her to free me
to unravel this madness
and finally see me
in all broken beauty
with all damaged parts
explosives have nothing
compared to these sparks

with the very last move, I finally dare
to ask her to enter this place inside where
I succumb to her wishes
I give up all control
devoured by her voracity, I become whole
her caresses so delicate
an evanescent challenge
which I fear to respond to
as if it might
                  vanish

her fingers are teasing
they go in and withdraw
I feel her breathing and releasing
this should be against the law
to arouse me and push me
up against a wall of *temptation*
to an almost unbearable expectation
of pleasure

her mouth eluding mine
she seeks every curve
and suddenly is still
leaving me unnerved
I am longing for fusion
in her every embrace
on every area of my body
she's leaving her trace
touching and then deserting it
a warm, trembling short circuit
so long delayed that when possession finally comes
it avenges the waiting, and *two* become *one*

I'm melting inside
rhythms flushing me up
deepening whirlpools of sensation erupt
through all my consciousness and into my heart
I open my eyes and give in to her dark

transgression

first transgressions into a world uncharted
that was unknown territory until this all started
a desert apparently only waiting to be fertilized
imagination leaves us hypnotized
messages between the lines

and the distance is fueling the fire in between
a vision   *a maybe*   a could-be   or a *dream*
projection imagining a bigger scheme
and it's probably anyhow not what it seems

so newly when I withdraw into myself
I can find you in ways that I just cannot help
I hadn't anticipated your touch and your smell
to have such a lively story to tell

fantasies of a naked slumber
are pulling me into these times of hunger
drink me up and fuck me blind
keep me sane, make me lose my mind

swept by the tempest of your love
I'm giving in
                    I'm giving up

see, my soul is a mix of chaos and art
and so I beg you to *kiss me apart*

jealousy

I want to give you freedom
like the one I pretend to own
while I'm chained by my desires
you out there
me here alone

I know I act
I act it out
I just sit
and wait
for everything is fleeting
love
beauty
even pain
I can't give it away
the fire that consumes me
makes me want to
        touch you
        seduce you
while I'm begging you to choose me
whenever you let me wait
and yet

I want you to engage
resign yourself to fate
embrace it
and have faith

I know I'm limited and helpless
  I want what I can't have
and then I swear I never wanted it
right in the aftermath

I guess I should have shown you
all my scars right from the start
but I'm painfully aware
that was always the most difficult part

the thing is
I've walked on
when I knew where this road led
and I bathed myself in misery
  of *all the things you never said*

but I dreamed them
I still dream them
they're in my head out loud
when there's no way to tomorrow
and all I do is silently shout

and all these cigarettes after sex
can't undo what has been done
the smoke in my lungs
cannot change
  I'm not the one

we're not *it*
and we can't be
never mind *consistency*

and so your face that says
    I told you so
can't console my shattered heart
cannot resolve this war inside
cannot kiss this mouth apart

and I don't even have it clear
what Disney princesses would like
it's all and everything the same
from every cake a little bite

so,
I think I take my chances
with forever
and let you in
I'll never have to wonder
where I end and you begin

I'll remain a soul at war with words
from battles waged within

a love affair

kiss me
she says
like I am the center of gravity
and you are falling into me
like my soul
is the focal point of yours

when I whisper
        I love you
what I really mean is
            I don't want you to leave

you taught me that
to be soft
is really to be powerful
and so I love
although
what are the odds
of me being really seen by you?

for every time I gift you poetry
I give away a part of me
lost in your silence
like a black hole
I guess it's true that
a muse is just a love affair
between art and a soul

confessions

every time I come walking out of the storm
still reeling from the neurotic and wrecked frenzy
that is the puzzling labyrinth of my mind
    I wonder
is this the scent of resolution?
or is retribution waiting for me around the next corner

I consciously fill up the space between us
convinced that I become whole not in relation to myself
but only through encountering the otherness
    I find in you
pushing boundaries until they almost burst
because my thirst for more is as voracious as it is torture

all journeys have secret destinations
of which the travelers are unaware
and I will always be a child of the wilderness
    wishing
that to taste the salt of friendship on my lips
would feel just a bit less bittersweet

so as I believe we can only be redeemed
to the extent to which we recognize ourselves
in our desperate attempts for tenderness
    I confess
that though I've never said it, I guess I never dared
love was there   in the silence

Inspired by

Beau Taplin **beautaplin.com**
Rupi Kaur **rupikaur.com**
Ruby Dhal **rubydhal.wordpress.com**
Atticus **atticuspoetry.com**
Danielle Doby **danielledoby.com**
David Jones **davidjoneswriter.com**
Janet Fitch **janetfitchwrites.com**
Octavio Paz
Anne Carson
Viktor E. Frankl
Stephen King
Jack Kerouac
Anaïs Nin

Kae Tempest **kaetempest.co.uk**
The Fray **thefray.com**
Billie Eilish **billieeilish.com**
Dermot Kennedy **dermotkennedy.com**
JP Cooper **jpcoopermusic.com**
U2 **u2.com**
Bob Dylan
Beethoven
Queen

Pablo Picasso

p. 17 'I learned to cultivate loneliness...'
    is inspired by Janet Fitch's 'White Oleander'

    'I'll choose empathy over disconnection...'
    is inspired by Danielle Doby's 'I Am Her Tribe'

    'nothing I've learned can prepare me,
    for everything else that needs learning'
    is a line from 'Firesmoke' by Kae Tempest

p. 18 'the lover wants what he can't have...'
    is inspired by Anne Carson's 'Eros the Bittersweet'

    'to love is to battle...'
    is inspired by Octavio Paz' 'Piedra de Sol'

    'gone for now, feels a lot like gone for good'
    is a line from 'Happiness' by The Fray

p.19 'let me break you so you can be open...'
    is inspired by Danielle Doby's 'I Am Her Tribe'

p. 20 'let this be more than just waiting...'
    is inspired by 'Bad Place for a Good Time' by Kae
    Temptest

p. 21 'I'm not driven by instinct, but drawn in by significance...'
    is inspired by Viktor E. Frankl's 'Der leidende Mensch'

    'is this the real life, or is it just fantasy?'
    is a line from 'Bohemian Rhapsody' by Queen

p. 66   'it's both a blessing and a curse to feel everything...'
         is a quote by David Jones

p. 68 ff the poem is inspired by the 4 cornerstones of eroticism
          by Dr. Jack Morin's 'The Erotic Mind'

p. 77   'call me friend but keep me closer'
         is a line from 'when the party's over' by Billie Eilish

p. 78   'hold me, thrill me, kiss me, kill me'
         is a song with the same title by U2

p. 80   'cause there's something in her tenderness that makes
         me want to live'

         'explosives have nothing compared to these sparks'
         are both lines from 'Firesmoke' by Kae Tempest

p. 82   'my soul is a mix of chaos and art'
         is a line inspired by the song 'Outnubered' by Dermot
         Kennedy

         'kiss me apart'
         is inspired by Beau Taplin's 'A Kiss'

p. 85   'a soul at war with words from battles waged within'

p. 86   'a muse is just a love affair between art and a soul'
         are quotes by Atticus' from 'The Dark between Stars'

p. 87   'love was there in the silence'
         is a line from JP Cooper's 'In the Silence'

Thank you

To express it in the words of Danielle Doby: Thank you to all my mirrors, my teachers, the technicolored souls in my life that pulled me out from my nest of hiding because they believed in the wild possibility that is me in this world. You pushed me, broke me, mended me, loved me, saved me and inspired me to keep reaching for more.

Thank you to Núria for intuitively understanding the nuances of my words and perfectly capturing them in a picture. Thank you to Sophie for translating my lines into another art form, to her brother, Jeremi, for his patience and creative support, and to Melanie for the finishing touch. Thank you to Jesh de Rox and Yrsa Daley-Ward for putting together a magical journey named Constellation and having me join their wild ride to the depth of ourselves. I might have never finished this book if it hadn't been for you.

And lastly, my sincerest thanks go to Michael, my rock, the love of a lifetime, endlessly supportive through all the messy intensity that comes with being engaged to a poet. Thank you. My ability to leap into the unknown is only due to the stability you're so generously providing.